D0581755

CATastrophes

First published in Great Britain in 2005
by PAST TIMES®, Oxford, England

Copyright ©2005 Complete Editions

Typeset by David Onyett, Publishing & Production Services,
Cheltenham
Cover and design by Peter Wilkinson
Illustrations courtesy of Mary Evans Picture Library
Printed in China by Imago

PAST TIMES

CATastrophes

A Little Light Relief

The actor Peter Ustinov decided to treat his daughter to her first live opera when she was still quite young. The performance he chose was a production of Verdi's magnificent *Aida*, which was being staged in the equally magnificent setting of the Baths of Caracalla in Rome.

The little girl was mesmerised by the experience until, during a pivotal scene, a number of stray cats who had made their home in the ancient ruins decided to relieve themselves simultaneously.

This was the moment when Peter Ustinov felt a light tapping at his elbow and heard a small voice asking, 'Daddy. Is it all right if I laugh?'

CATastrophes

Artistic Licence

In the spring of 2002 the celebrated artist, Tracy Emin, suffered the anxiety dreaded by all pet owners when her cat, Docket, went missing.

Desperate to find Docket, she dashed off a number of home-made posters and displayed them around the immediate neighbourhood, appealing for information.

To her dismay and disappointment, the posters were quickly torn down; though not through any dislike of Docket, or Miss Emin. In fact the opposite proved to be the case. Although an assistant had commented that the poster design was 'not a conceptual piece of work', others spotted what they saw as a chance to make some easy money. Word went round that the posters were worth £500 each and down they came.

The happy end to the story is that, although the posters disappeared, Docket did not, and was later reunited with its much relieved owner.

Cat Sanctuary

The Revd Stephen Hawker, who served as the vicar of Mortenstow in Cornwall during the middle years of the nineteenth century, had a remarkable empathy with animals and was especially devoted to cats.

One of these was a young male cat named Grandfer who developed the peculiar, and somewhat tiresome, habit of 'retrieving' smaller wildlife and bringing them into the parsonage house.

CATastrophes

'In Spring,' Hawker wrote to a friend, 'when he finds a bird's nest, he brings the young ones up in his mouth, one at a time, and drops them unhurt by my chair. A whole nest of the large-sized tom-tit that he so served were carried back, and lived to fly away, Grandfer being shut up till they fledged. He has brought up a young mole and a frog – a most intelligent cat.'

Though perhaps only an ardent cat lover would view such behaviour quite so indulgently.

CATastrophes

In a Spin

Dr Bastin and his family were the proud owners of Monty, a magnificent five-year-old colour point Persian cat.

Theirs was a busy household that was always a hive of activity. One day Monty sauntered into the garage looking for a little peace and quiet, which found him inside the open door of the tumble dryer.

He was nodding off when a pile of sheets and pillowcases was suddenly shoved on top of him, the door closed and the most nightmarish thirty-five minutes of Monty's nine lives began.

It was only when the family noticed that

the tumble-dryer sounded different that the doctor went to investigate and heard faint miaows. When the door was opened and the bed linen pulled out, Dr Bastin was greeted by the sight of a very groggy Monty who had been tumbled for over half an hour through thousands of revolutions.

With medical quick thinking, the doctor realised the cat was running a high temperature and took prompt action to cool him down, first with ice cubes and then with an unceremonious dunking in a bowl of water.

Poor Monty was less than amused, but when his ordeal was over, he was wrapped in a towel and placed in the sun to dry. He made a full recovery in a couple of days, but avoided the garage ever afterwards.

CATastrophes

Oysters for the Cat

James Boswell, friend and biographer of Samuel Johnson, loathed cats. However, since Johnson was devoted to them, Boswell kept his feelings to himself and let readers decide for themselves what he thought about his friend's obsession with them.

'I shall never forget,' wrote Boswell, 'the indulgence with which he treated Hodge, his cat; for whom he himself used to go out and buy oysters, lest the servants having that trouble should take a dislike to the poor creature.'

White House Etiquette

A guest staying at the White House during the presidency of Calvin Coolidge at the end of the 1920s was slightly on edge at the prospect of breakfasting with the president.

CATastrophes

Coolidge was a notoriously taciturn man, with no time for small talk. This the guest was prepared for. What threw him completely was seeing the president pouring some milk from his cup into a saucer.

Anxious that he might be about to breach some obscure White House etiquette if he didn't follow suit, the guest poured some milk into his own saucer.

The president said nothing. He merely bent down and placed the saucer of milk on the floor for the cat, which had entered the room and had been sitting unobserved at its master's feet.

Breakfast continued in an even heavier silence after this.

Murka's Mystery Miles

Murka, a black and white cat living in Moscow, was banished to the home of her owner's relatives 400 miles away, after she unlatched the door of a birdcage and killed the two canaries inside.

Her stay in her new home lasted just two days before she disappeared. A year later her former owner noticed a cat that looked very like the killer of his canaries outside his apartment building. Closer inspection of the dirty and heavily pregnant cat confirmed that Murka had indeed somehow succeeded in making the 400-mile trek home to Moscow.

Apart from needing a good clean and plenty to eat, and in due course raising her kittens, the only evidence of her ordeal was the missing tip of her tail. In every other respect Moscow Murka seemed completely untroubled by her extraordinary adventure.

The Final Insult

Cats who quail at the prospect of being put in the dog house would be well advised to avoid the Oxford Union building where a time-honoured statute decrees, 'No dog shall be allowed to enter the premises unless accompanying a blind person, in which case it shall be deemed to be a cat.'

Sweet Dreams

A Birmingham cat named Cindy curled up in her favourite armchair at home and sank into a blissful sleep. When Cindy woke up, things were different. She was still in the armchair, but the sitting-room had somehow been changed into a large dark rattling box filled with piled-up furniture and cardboard boxes.

The furniture van she had been travelling in had also just pulled up outside a new home in Southampton.

Where There's A Will

Cats have not infrequently been the beneficiaries of wills left by their doting owners – and not always with the complete agreement of human relatives.

In September 1944, a lawyer in Brooklyn left over £25,000 to his cat, thereby cutting out five relatives 'because of their contemptuous attitude towards the cat'.

In 1917 a wealthy Austrian woman, Mathilde Kovacs, burned her entire fortune just before her death – because her next of kin had been unfriendly towards her cats and consequently she didn't want her heartless relatives to enjoy any of her fortune.

Spiting the unkind (and therefore unworthy) is not the only time that cats benefit from the estate of

their owners. In the second half of the eighteenth century the French harpist Madame Dupuis made careful provision for the well-being of her cats after her death, though imposing considerable demands on her surviving relatives at the same time...

'*Item:* I desire my sister, Marie Bluteau, and my niece, Madame Calonge, to look to my cats. If both should survive me, thirty sous a week must be laid out upon them, in order that they may live well.

'They are to be served daily, in a clean and proper manner, with two meals of soup, the same as we eat ourselves, but it is to be given to them separately in two soup-plates. The bread is not to be cut in to the soup, but must be broken into squares about the size of a nut, otherwise they will refuse to eat it. A ration of meat, finely minced, is to be added to it; the whole is then to be mildly seasoned, put into a clean pan, covered close, and carefully simmered before it is dished up. If only one cat should survive, half the sum mentioned will suffice.

'Nicole-Page is to take charge of my two cats, and to be very careful to them. Madame Calonge to visit them three times a week.'

A Fishy Tale

'A shopkeeper in Barbados ran what you would call a corner-shop in England, which sold a variety of goods to anyone who was willing and able to buy,' Barbados High Commissioner Roy Marshall once recalled. 'He was assisted by his wife and family and supported by a variety of cats which he kept ostensibly to protect his wares from the ravages of mice and the like.

'On one occasion I was in the shop when a woman burst in, complaining angrily about the depredations of one of the cats which she alleged had stolen

CATastrophes

and eaten the five pounds of fish that she had purchased for her family's dinner.

'Without batting an eyelid, the shopkeeper pointed to a corner, where a cat was dozing contentedly, and asked, "Lady, is that the cat?"

'"Yes," she replied, whereupon he went over, picked up the cat, brought it back to the counter and put it on the scales which weighed in at just over five pounds.

'"Lady," asked the shopkeeper, "if that is your fish, where the hell is my cat!?"'

Psycatry

Cats who take after their owners may not always reflect mankind to the best. That at least was the conclusion of a correspondent to the *Nottingham Evening Post* who shared with fellow readers this uncompromising opinion . . .

'With regard to damage done by cats, and gardens contaminated, etc., all this is psychological. Such cats are a reflection of the homes they come from as we all are.'

Seven Up

CATastrophes

Buster was cat with a canny sense of self-preservation. Far from pining for his owner when he was on holiday, Buster went on an eating binge which resulted in his having to be put on a crash diet. Though this only happened when Buster's rapidly expanding waistline was explained by the fact that he was greedily downing seven breakfasts, seven lunches and seven suppers every day.

It turned out that seven members of his owner's staff had individually taken to feeding the boss's cat, because they felt sorry for him and concluded that he hadn't been fed.

Where Buster was clever was in approaching each individual when he or she was alone; never when they were with one or more other members of staff. And so he continued his happy round of dining until the size of his tummy finally gave him away.

CATastrophes

The Cat that Got the Cream

When she died in 1975, Ivy Blackhurst, of Sheffield, left £20,000 in her will to her cat Blackie. Blackie followed her mistress to the next world in 1978 at the impressive age of eighteen, but not before she had spent the intervening three years enjoying the run of

CATastrophes

Mrs Blackhurst's detached house where she was waited on by a full-time housekeeper.

Let Sleeping Cats Lie

The French medical missionary, Dr Albert Schweitzer, who dedicated more than fifty years of his life to administering to the population of a remote region of French Equatorial Guinea, adored animals. During his time in Africa he had a cat named Sizi of whom he was inordinately fond.

Schweitzer was left-handed but he had to get into the habit of writing with his right hand as well as his left. The reason for becoming ambidextrous was Sizi. She took to sleeping on his left arm when he was working and when Sizi slept, she could not be disturbed.

CATastrophes

Devil's Familiar

Sir Francis Dashwood was the eighteenth-century founder of the notorious Hell-Fire Club, whose members met in a 'church' decorated with obscene carvings where they took part in licentious goings-on dressed as monks and nuns.

Sir Francis blamed his peculiar pastime, not unreasonably, on the devil, whom he claimed to have seen and heard. From this chilling encounter stemmed Sir Francis's conversion to Satanism.

Unfortunately for Sir Francis the lord of the underworld had not in fact chosen to pay a visit to the Dashwood home. The 'devil' that had made such a lasting impression on Sir Francis was in fact two cats intimately enjoying each other's company in the night.

CATastrophes

Milk Round

A farm cat, from the days when milk was still collected in churns, got into the habit of waiting for the milk lorry to come and one day went missing after the lorry's departure.

The lorry continued on its circuitous route, collecting churns from one farm after another and at the end of the run returned to the depot. Here the churns were unloaded and sleeping snugly between the last three was the farm cat. However, the cat had no intention of being caught, so leapt from the lorry and disappeared.

Luckily the driver remembered the cat waiting for him and pinpointed the farm where it lived. The next morning he told the cowman what had happened, but neither man thought there was any chance of ever seeing the cat again.

Fifteen days later, a very bedraggled cat limped with bleeding paws into its former home. Somehow it had covered the twelve miles from the milk depot, without any prior knowledge of how to find its way home.

CATastrophes

It was half-starved, but it was safe – and it never went near the milk lorry again.

Basket Case

Although the celebrated actress Edith Evans made her name in the classical theatre, she counted a number of memorable film roles among her successes. Among these was her portrayal of Betsey Trotwood in the screen adaptation of *David Copperfield*.

During one scene she had to carry a cat in a basket on her arm. As setting the scene and positioning the lights and cameras took some time, it was thought wise to sedate the cat to avoid any unscripted antics.

When the cameras were rolling and Dame Edith was well into a lengthy speech, there were stirrings in the basket; the sedative was beginning to wear off.

Barely pausing in her delivery and with no

CATastrophes

indication of distraction, Dame Edith pushed the cat back into the basket, hissing to it, 'Don't be such an ambitious pussy. You're not in *Dick Whittington*.'

CATastrophes

A Tale of Two Cats

Anyone familiar with the popular television series *Blackadder* will recognise the significance of the name Baldrick that was given to a cat who was invariably untidy.

CATastrophes

Baldrick lived with his lady owner and enjoyed a comfortable, if not terribly active life judging by his girth. His habits were regular, though. After an early morning breakfast, he would take a nap on his owner's bed before slipping out around midday. By mid-afternoon he was home again ready for another meal.

And so Baldrick's life continued until the time when he suddenly vanished for three weeks. When he finally returned one leg was in splints and plaster. Baldrick had evidently had a nasty accident and some kind person had seen to it that he was cared for.

His owner was anxious to find out who this was. Some enquiries revealed another lady who lived not too far away. Baldrick's owner called round to thank her only to be told, 'But that's my cat!'

Baldrick, it appeared, had two homes, two owners, two names (he was known as Scruffy in the second house) and double rations! However, his two owners were so amused by his antics that they continued with their cat's unconventional lifestyle – with one exception. From then on he had to make do with smaller portions of food.

A Christmas Carol

Tragedy struck a family in Chard, Somerset, over Christmas 1985. After tucking into his festive dinner, Tigger, the family cat, simply disappeared.

Searches of the neighbourhood over several weeks produced no sign of him and his heartbroken owners resigned themselves to his loss. In time they were joined by another cat, named Max, but Tigger lived long in their memories.

Then in September 1991, six years later, a neighbour noticed a cat bearing a striking resemblance to Tigger sitting on her fence. The family of the lost cat

CATastrophes

checked for themselves and realised from the scars on its nose that their missing pet had miraculously returned.

Their only conclusion was that Tigger must have been accidentally driven off in the family car, where he liked to take a nap, and had been making his way home ever since.

Happily for all concerned, Tigger settled into his old routine quite contentedly and best of all Max appeared to show no signs of resentment at his unexpected arrival.

Rent-A-Kitty

The author Mark Twain was devoted to cats and was never happy when he had to spend time away from them. Late in life he took a holiday in New Hampshire, which threatened to be a disaster because of the great man's pining for his pets at home.

CATastrophes

The holiday was salvaged by a timely visit to a nearby farm. Here Mark Twain succeeded in renting kittens to keep him company until he returned home.

Cat, Book and Candle

Charles Dickens was not always a lover of cats. At first no cats were allowed in his home for fear of what they might do to the birds already domiciled in the house. However, all this changed when his daughter, Williamina, was given a white kitten that shared her name.

This cat, like so many others, had a way of wheedling her way into people's affections. Before long she (and the cats that followed her example) were ruling the house and getting away it, as this recollection of her young mistress shows.

'I remember on one occasion when she had presented us with a family of kittens, she selected a corner of father's study for their home. She brought them one by one from the kitchen and deposited them in her chosen corner. My father called to me to remove them, saying that he could not allow the kittens to remain in his room. I did so, but Williamina brought them back again, one by one. Again they were removed. The third time, instead of putting them in the

CATastrophes

corner, she placed them all, and herself beside them, at my father's feet, and gave him such an imploring glance that he could resist no longer, and they were allowed to remain. As the kittens grew older they became more and more frolicsome, swarming up the curtains, playing about on the writing table and scampering behind the book shelves. But they were never complained of and lived happily in the study until the time came for finding them other homes.

'One of these kittens was kept, who, as he was quite deaf, was left unnamed, and became known by the servants as "the master's cat", because of his devotion to my father. He was always with him, and used to follow him about the garden like a dog, and sit with him while he wrote. One evening we were all, except father, going to a ball, and when we started, left "the master" and his cat in the drawing-room together. "The master" was reading at a small table, on which a lighted candle was placed. Suddenly the candle went out. My father, who was much interested in his book, relighted the candle, stroked the cat, who was looking at him pathetically he noticed, and continued his reading. A few minutes later, as the light became dim, he looked up just in time to see puss deliberately put out the candle with his paw, and then look appealingly toward him. This second and unmistakable hint was not disregarded, and puss was given the petting he craved. Father was full of this anecdote when all met at breakfast the next morning.'

Copy Cat

During the 1930s the author Raymond Chandler owned a black Persian cat called Taki. Chandler was devoted to Taki and frequently referred to her in terms that would make anyone unfamiliar with his domestic arrangements believe that Taki was human.

The confusion was even more understandable when Chandler called her his secretary. There was a good reason for this. It was not uncommon for Taki to sit on paper her master was about to write on, or even to plant herself on copy that needed revising.

CATastrophes

Tamar Tommy

When the family cat, Tommy, was discovered stranded and terrified on the 150-foot-high Tamar Bridge that links Devon and Cornwall, thirteen-year-old Jason

Snell took it on himself to rescue it.

While a crowd gathered to watch, Jason scaled a fifty-foot wall and then crawled up a one-hundred-foot angled girder before walking along a narrow gangway below the road bridge to reach the cat.

Tommy was rigid with fear, but must have recognised Jason, because

he allowed himself to be tucked inside his coat for the perilous descent.

When he reached the ground again, Jason was given a sound ticking off by police officers for taking such a risk. As the boy explained, though, no one else would have stood a chance of rescuing Tommy. In spite of his predicament, the cat would have scratched them to pieces, he explained.

All the President's Cats

In the early years of the nineteenth century Theodore Roosevelt occupied the White House as the twenty-sixth president of the United States and his cats revelled in their new status as the nation's number one pets.

One of Roosevelt's cats, named Slippers, took to his new surroundings with even greater ease than the president's other cats and was soon lounging and relaxing wherever he chose in the nation's most exclusive address. On one occasion Slippers was found sprawled extravagantly right in the middle of the hall that links the state drawing-room with the dining-room.

Slippers was fully aware of his importance and therefore completely ignored the distinguished guests dining with the president that night. As they processed into dinner, Slippers held his ground and refused to budge, even when the line of advancing diners was obliged to change direction and walk round him.

Catch Me If You Can

Pet lovers in New York were horrified to read reports that 132 cats had been dropped seven storeys into the streets below – amazingly only three had died.

The truth, as investigated by the city's Animal Medical Center, proved to be rather different. None of

CATastrophes

the cats had in fact been dropped from high rise build-
ings, as claimed. They had all either jumped or
accidentally fallen out of windows and all but the
unhappy three had been amazingly lucky. One cat had

CATastrophes

actually fallen thirty-two storeys and survived with just bruises to its chest and lungs, and a chipped tooth.

War Victims

In times of war deserted cats may struggle for the attention of any human beings, let alone heads of state, but this was not the case with Abraham Lincoln, a president noted for his compassion in war and peace.

In the course of the American Civil War, Lincoln was visiting General Grant's camp when he came across three motherless kittens in a tent. Despite the many demands placed on the president at the time, Lincoln gathered up the three miserable creatures and took them into the warmth and comfort of his coat and kept them there until he made certain that they could be properly cared for.

CATastrophes

CATastrophes

Missing Presumed Dead

In the early years of the twentieth century a cat known to the staff of the British Museum as 'Black Jack' became a frequent visitor to Sir Richard Garnett, who was in charge of the museum's famous Department of Printed Books. The archaeologist and writer, Sir Ernest A. Wallis, recorded what happened next.

'He was fond of sitting on the desks in the Reading Room, and he never hesitated to ask a reader to hold open both folding doors when he wanted to go out into the corridor. Being shut in one of the newspaper rooms one Sunday, and being bored, he amused himself by sharpening his claws on the bindings of the volumes of newspapers, and it must be confessed, did much damage. This brought down upon him the wrath of the officials, and he was banished from the library; the Clerk of the Works was ordered to get rid of him, and tried to do so, but failed, for Black

Jack had disappeared mysteriously. The truth was that two of the members of the staff arranged for him to be kept in safety in a certain place, and provided him with food and milk. An official report was written to the effect that Black Jack had disappeared, and he was "presumed dead"; the bindings of the volumes of newspapers were repaired, and the official mind was once more at peace. A few weeks later Black Jack reappeared, and everyone was delighted to see him again; and the chief officials asked no questions!'

The Emperor and the Kitten

Fearless on the battlefield and a general who commanded the admiration and respect of the tens of thousands of men who served under him, Napoleon Bonaparte was not a man to be heard crying for help in the middle of the night. So an aide was very alarmed

CATastrophes

one night during a campaign to hear the emperor's voice raised in terror calling for help.

The aide rushed into the room to be met by the alarming sight of Napoleon half dressed and sweating heavily, lunging with his sword through the tapestry lining the walls.

The aide drew his own sword and went in search of the assailant. Behind the tapestry he found a tiny kitten.

CATastrophes

Road Cat's Eyes

The Italian racing driver Alberto Ascari was well known for being extremely superstitious. He would avoid ill omens at any expense and lived in dread of the number 13. Black cats were a particular phobia for him and on one occasion he came across a black cat in the road and promptly turned his car round and continued his journey by another route to avoid crossing the path taken by the cat.

Nine Lives Morris

A cat named Morris became the famous finicky star of commercials for a brand of cat food named 9-Lives. Indeed as his career developed, Morris was assigned round-the-clock security guards to prevent his kidnap and subsequent blackmail attempts on the company.

CATastrophes

In Morris's case, 9-Lives was a more than suitable name for the product that ensured his livelihood.

CATastrophes

Before he was rescued and subsequently entered the glittering showbiz career that made him famous, Morris had been taken as a stray to an animal shelter in Chicago, where he was just twenty minutes away from being destroyed.

As a mark of his good fortune, his picture was proudly hung on the wall of the local animal pound.

Cat Litter

Mitzi was a cat who could not abide litter. School children on their way home were often tailed by the cat, which picked up discarded sweet wrappers and crisp packets.

This concern for keeping the streets clean was all very well, but one day Mitzi went too far. To her owner's confusion and embarrassment she deposited two ten-pound notes and two fivers in their garden –

CATastrophes

money she had picked up from a house five doors away, where she had slipped in through a bedroom window.

Cat Overboard

Eighteenth-century seamen were not noted for being tender-hearted, but the novelist Henry Fielding witnessed a remarkable contradiction of this assumption during a voyage to Lisbon in July 1754.

One of the ship's cats, a kitten, tumbled from a cabin window and fell into the sea. The moment word reached the captain, he ordered the crew to slow the ship, so that steps could be taken to rescue the poor creature.

The odds on the kitten's survival looked long indeed, which made the captain's actions all the more remarkable in Fielding's eyes. Even so, the quick-witted boatswain tore off his jacket, shirt and breeches and leapt over the side. A few minutes later he swam back to the ship holding the kitten's lifeless body in his mouth.

The poor little animal was laid on the deck in the sunlight but showed every sign of having drowned. The captain, as Fielding recorded, 'declared he had rather have lost a cask of rum or brandy'.

CATastrophes

However, his kindness was not in vain. Against all appearances the kitten rallied and in time was restored to full health. The captain was delighted; his crew less so. Sailors are notoriously superstitious and many aboard Fielding's ship grumbled that the kitten had been saved. As far as they were concerned, drowning a cat was the surest way of raising a favourable wind.

Identity Crisis

At times the American nightclub singer and entertainer, Wayne Newton, has owned half-a-dozen cats and his obsession with his feline companions has led to some unlikely occurrences. One of his cats, Annie, became convinced that she was a dog and took to growling instead of the more familiar miaowing practised by her companions. She needed treatment by a therapist to help her resolve this identity crisis.

CATastrophes

Then, towards the end of 1999, Wayne Newton was persuaded to act as a judge in a strange contest held in Florida. This was the only time in his career that he ever agreed to judge anything. What swung his decision on this occasion was the bizarre nature of the

competition. Cat owners who entered (as only cat owners would in the circumstances) were required to sing the advertising jingle to a line of cat food called Miaow Mix.

One by one they solemnly took the stage and sang, 'Miaow, miaow, miaow, miaow, miaow, miaow...'

Votes for Cats

The democratic process faced a new challenge when a householder in Southend filed the names of his two cats as electors in a local election.

The cats in question, Porky and Tim, were issued with voting cards and poll numbers for the local government election to be held in Southend East. Their owner, Mr Robin Mist, had filled in a Register of Electors form in the names of the cats. By way of explanation, Mr Mist claimed he intended to leave

CATastrophes

everything to his cats, and as they would be house-holders they deserved to have a vote.

CATastrophes

Bank Interest

Domingo was a Blue Point Balinese and the prized pet of a lady in Devon. She was devastated when he disappeared and no amount of searching produced any sign of him.

Some two months later staff at a local bank noticed unusual noises at the back of their strong room. This was searched, but without discovering the source of the noise, which could still be heard.

Next to the strong room was a cellar, where a very bedraggled cat was found and identified as Domingo by the name tag he was wearing. It appeared that the cat had fallen down the forty-foot cliff behind the bank and had found its way into the cellar. How he had survived for eight weeks was remarkable, but survive he did.

CATastrophes

From Your Own Correspondent

In 1957 Howard Hughes, the famous American aviator and businessman, married Jean Peters, who in time formed a close attachment to a scruffy and physically unprepossessing tomcat.

CATastrophes

One day this cat went missing and with his wife's anxious urging, Hughes took control of a search and rescue operation. Dozens of people were drafted in to find the missing moggy. Hughes set up rescue headquarters in his home and demanded hourly progress reports.

In the end the cat was traced to a derelict barn, where it was apprehended, so that Hughes could take a good look at it. He was less than impressed and swiftly decided that this particular cat would not be an appropriate addition to the Hughes household.

He interviewed several families willing to adopt the cat, but none met with his approval. So the cat was lodged in a luxurious cattery. Here it lived in an individually decorated room complete with television. Not that Hughes's obligations to the cat stopped there. One of the conditions of residence was that former owners were expected to write to their pets at least once a month. Too busy and frankly unwilling to do this himself, Howard Hughes engaged an Australian named Harry to write the monthly letters to the cat. When Howard Hughes died in 1976 Harry was still drawing his salary.

Nietzsche and the Man from Mars

The Canadian singer–songwriter, Joni Mitchell, had an interesting experience with her cat, which led to an unforeseen result, as she later explained.

'My cat, Nietzsche got mad at me about something, and he got up on this chair and he peed right close to my ear. He jumped off from there and ran with his belly to the floor. He knew he did wrong. I caught up to him and I took him by the tip of his tail and the scruff of the neck and I held him at arm's length so he couldn't scratch me, because he's really strong.

CATastrophes

CATastrophes

'I said, "O.K., if you're going to act like an animal, you can live like an animal."

'I put him outside for the night, which I would never do. Well, he's very sensitive, you know. I hurt his feelings. And he didn't come back the first night. He didn't come back the second night. I only had a picture of him as a kitten. So I painted him, had it photographed, and on the third day took it to the printer, and got it back in laminate form on the fifth day, and hand-delivered it into everybody's mailbox in a three-mile radius. On the back it said, "Have you seen my Nietzsche?" and gave the phone number to call.

'He was gone for eighteen days, and like a method actor I took the pain of his absence and wrote the song "Man from Mars". Even in the mix you can hear it. I had been out there listening for him and my ear was hearing three miles away. It is the deepest mix that I ever did, with little sounds going way, way, way back into the mix . . .

'So I finished the song. It took me seventeen days, and on the eighteenth day he came back. He stayed away just long enough for me to write.'